GUIDES TO EVERYTHING

# 25 WAYS TO BOOST YOUR INCOME

By Emma Lunn

ISBN 978-1-84678-007-3

Copyright 2006, Quick123 Limited

Quick123 Limited, PO Box 45092, London N4 2ZJ.

Website: www.quick123.co.uk

Customer service or additional copies can be sought at service@quick123.co.uk.

Published by Quick123 Ltd. Reproduction of all or any part of this publication without prior written permission of the publisher is strictly prohibited. While every precaution has been taken to ensure that the information in this publication is true and accurate, the publisher assumes no responsibility for errors or omissions. This publication is not intended to replace professional advice.

• QUICK123 GUIDES TO EVERYTHING •

# Letter to the Reader

Most of us find ourselves a bit short of cash from time to time. That could be because we are saving for holidays, a car or a deposit on a house or just because we're keen to pay off a credit card bill.

Whether you're a student, pensioner, parent, working full-time, part-time or not at all, there are numerous ways of boosting your income. The best 25 of them are listed in this guide. Some require skills, others time and some imagination.

I have done a number of the things outlined. While a student, I took advantage of cheap course fees on offer and became a qualified swimming teacher.

Once I was qualified, teaching brought in more money than the typical student jobs – working in bars or shops – and was much more rewarding.

• QUICK123 GUIDES TO EVERYTHING •

After university, I had debts to clear: as well as a temp job as a receptionist, I also worked three nights a week in a city bar. It ended up being great fun, a good way to meet people and was generally much more enjoyable than my day job. It also brought in about £60 to £70 a week.

Since then, when times have been tight I have offered my body – to science. I've taken part in a memory experiment and have identified different smells while lying in a scanner having my brain activity assessed.

These will give you a flavour of some of the ideas contained in this guide. There are plenty more outlined here, along with the information you need to go out and try them.

Happy boosting!

*Emma Luna*

# Contents

| | |
|---|---|
| **How to boost your income** | 1 |
| **Get rich quick...** | 4 |
| **THE 25 WAYS - Time on your hands** | 9 |
| **THE 25 WAYS - Sell, sell, sell** | 19 |
| **THE 25 WAYS - Use your body** | 23 |
| **THE 25 WAYS - Space to spare** | 29 |
| **THE 25 WAYS - What you've got** | 34 |
| **THE 25 WAYS - Use your skills** | 38 |
| **THE 25 WAYS - Use your imagination** | 44 |
| **Another approach** | 49 |
| **And finally** | 55 |
| **Further reading** | 56 |

• QUICK123 GUIDES TO EVERYTHING •

Quick123 Limited
PO Box 45092
London N4 2ZJ

Email: peterpurton@quick123.co.uk

# Dear Quick123 reader

Thank you for buying this guide. We hope you enjoy reading it.

Our aim is to help you achieve the goals you set yourself, whether it's getting a better job, improving relationships or creating a better you. And to help you achieve that without costing you too much time, effort or money.

Because you, the reader, are at the centre of everything we do, we'd like to hear from you. Whether you have comments about this book, ideas for a new topic or issues in your life you feel we might be able to help with, send us an email or a letter.

If we take up any of your ideas to create a new title we'll make sure you get your own special copy.

We want to provide you with the kinds of guides you want to read. With your help, I'm sure we can.

Happy reading,

Peter Purton
Quick123 Limited

# How to boost your income

Those of us not on fat-cat executive pay or receiving six-figure city bonuses find, increasingly, that our salary is not enough to live on. That is, if we have a salary at all.

A study by the Joseph Rowntree Foundation found that, although government policies had cut the number of families living in poverty, most workers in low paid jobs still don't earn enough to allow them to rely on their wages alone. The research classed almost one in four workers as 'low-paid'.

According to Payfinder (www.payfinder.com), the national average salary is £22,411; in many regions, workers earn less. Among those at the bottom of the pay scale are workers in the east of England, Wales and the south-west. Employees in some of these regions suffer both from low salaries and a relatively high cost of living.

As well as workers on low pay, other sectors of the population, such as students and pensioners, often need an extra bob or two. Students typically graduate with debts of £13,680, according to Natwest, yet start work on an average salary of just £14,090.

Undergraduates rely increasingly on part time jobs to finance their life at university: 39 per cent of students have a part time job. Thinking outside the box and following some of the ideas here will help them boost their income without having to sacrifice their studies because they have to hold down a demanding job at the same time.

Many people look forward to retirement as a time when they will no longer have any money worries. In reality it is not all cruises and eating out once you collect your pension. Retirement property company, Economic Lifestyle, reckons that one in five pensioners lives below the poverty line.

Some of the money-making schemes outlined here can easily be put into practice by pensioners. They will be able to boost their retirement income and live the relaxed lifestyle they have always dreamed about.

# "Retirement is not all cruises and eating out...one in five pensioners lives below the poverty line"

25 ways to BOOST your income

# Get rich

• • • • • • • • • • • • • • • • • • • • • • • • • • • • •

If spending a little time and effort working your way through the ideas in this book seems like too much hassle, you might well be attracted by money making scams and 'get rich quick' schemes. These could be online or offline and take various forms. But don't be fooled; they are rarely what they seem.

Last year, following a sweep of the internet, the Office of Fair Trading (OFT) found numerous websites hosting 'too good to be true' offers. They included 90 'working from home' schemes, 52 'get rich quick' schemes and 20 lottery scams.

Among the shady operators the OFT uncovered were one 'get rich quick' site promising users they could make nearly £200,000 in one day and one home working scheme that offered 'business

# quick

• • • • • • • • • • • • • • • • • • • • • • • • • • •

opportunities' to make £2,500 a month. The sites remained strangely silent on exactly what anyone signing up had to do to rake in the cash.

Most scammers were found to be liberal with the truth on earning potential and also charged consumers 'joining fees'.

No one is going to give you untold riches for doing next to nothing so you would be best advised to ignore promises of instant wealth and 'free gifts'. If any of the schemes you come across seem worth a second look, make sure you research the business, verify contact details and read terms and conditions carefully before parting with money.

Many internet scam schemes fall into the 'network marketing' category, otherwise known as trading

**Get rich quick**
SPECIAL FEATURE

schemes or multi-level marketing. Trading schemes are a legitimate form of business activity offering individuals the opportunity to earn money by selling the scheme's goods or services from home.

In some schemes, participants may earn commission by recruiting others to the scheme. They become illegal when, while purporting to trade in goods or services, they aim to generate money by recruiting new participants. This is often referred to as 'pyramid selling'; efforts are concentrated on the recruitment of sales people rather than actual sales of a product.

The Department of Trade and Industry has issued a guidance booklet, 'The Trading Scheme Guide'. It explains current legislation and the questions participants should get answered before agreeing to take part in such a scheme.

Other pyramid schemes don't even pretend to sell goods and just claim to be a quick way to make some easy money. In a typical pyramid scheme, a potential member is asked to pay to join.

**Get rich quick**
SPECIAL FEATURE

The only way to advance is to recruit others, who also pay to join. If enough new members join, the pyramid will grow, possibly enabling some participants to make money. However, in order for every participant to make money, there needs to be an endless supply of newcomers.

A more modern scheme is an email-based scam. This is a form of 'advance fee fraud', often known as an 'African email' because this is the country where some of the scams are thought to originate. The scam often refers to a major event or misfortune, such as the overthrow of a government.

This event is claimed to have caused a large sum of money to have become 'trapped' in the troubled country. The individual or group concerned now seeks help in transferring that money to another country. A proportion of the money is offered in return for help with the transfer.

The sender then goes on to ask for your bank details and asks for an upfront fee to get

# Get rich quick
**SPECIAL FEATURE**

yourself involved. Inevitably, having parted with the money, you will never hear from your African business partner again.

Some people have had personal and company bank accounts emptied of money. It goes without saying that you should *never* reveal your bank or personal details to strangers.

In another form of shady scheme, people are told that they have won a prize draw, lottery or windfall. The notification may come either in the post or via email.

While some of these approaches are legitimate, others are a dishonest attempt to trap you into parting with your money. Often, access to a winning ticket, prize in an overseas draw or lottery or membership of a lottery syndicate, is only granted in return for payment of an 'administration' or 'registration' fee.

Just remember if something seems too good to be true, it probably is.

# THE 25 WAYS Time on your hands?

1. **Make money from your hobby**

   If you're interested in antiques, pottery, sewing or model making, turning your hobby into a money spinning idea could be for you. For example, if you make clothes or regularly alter them for friends, advertising your services in the local press or fabric shop can kick start your business.

   Likewise, if pottery is your passion, take examples along to craft shops, along with a brief summary of your history, and persuade them to stock your work. Although it may get off to a slow start, selling things you've made gives you the chance to make some cash while putting your creative and practical skills to good use.

## How much can you make?
This depends on what you are selling and how much your work is respected. Dress making pays between £5 and £10 an hour, while ceramic goods sell from £5 upwards.

## Contacts
www.studiopottery.com contains useful information for new and established potters.

www.fashion.arts.ac.uk is the website for the London College of Fashion and has details of short courses for fashion design and workshops for jewellery, knitwear and textiles.

The British Antique Dealers Association (www.bada.org) on 020 7589 4128 has details of antique dealers and fairs.

## 2. Tutoring
Whether you are a musical supremo, mathematical genius or are multi-lingual, the chances are that you have got a skill you can

**THE 25 WAYS: Time on your hands?**

## Case study

Sarah Keeler, 23, is a PR executive from Manchester. She makes and sells cards and jewellery in her spare time. "It's something I've always done since I was quite young," says Sarah, "but it's only in the last couple of years that I have started selling them."

Sarah sells the greetings cards and jewellery at craft stalls at weekends and normally spends about five hours a week on this way of boosting her income.

"I make a bit of extra cash doing it and I really enjoy it," she says, "normally I make about £80 at each craft fair I do."

teach others. Knowledge of the national curriculum can help if you approach local schools with English or maths skills.

Adverts in newsagents' windows are a way of attracting interest from people wanting to learn a musical instrument or language.

• QUICK123 GUIDES TO EVERYTHING •

Although you need to be patient, tutoring can be fun and rewarding.

### How much can you make?
Most private tutors charge between £10 and £20 per hour, depending on the subject and their level of qualifications.

### Contacts
www.anysubject.com lists tutors by subject and location and is a good place to advertise your services.

3. **Working in the evenings**
Pubs, restaurants and nightclubs often want part-time staff to work a couple of evenings during the week. They tend to advertise in their window or you can simply pop in and ask to speak to the manager.

The more experience you have, the better; but even novices should be able to pick up bar or waiting work easily enough and earn a bit of extra cash.

**THE 25 WAYS: Time on your hands?**

## Case study

Katie Richardson, 21, works at a PR company in London during the week but spends her Sundays working in the bar at a golf club near her home in Colchester. She says: "I've worked there on and off since I was 15, at weekends and in the university holidays. I don't get paid much for my day job and I earn about £35 a week from the bar. It's paid weekly and comes in useful.

"It's completely different from my day job which is in an office and, although it's tiring working six days a week, I really value having Saturdays off."

### How much can you make?

Wages are traditionally low in the hospitality industry, but you are also likely to get tips. Qualified chefs can earn upwards of £7 /hr.

### Contacts

www.reed.co.uk/hospitality lists bar, restaurant and catering jobs.

### 4. Mystery shopping

Shopping, and getting paid for it, sounds like

many people's dream job: there are companies out there that will pay you to do just that. They might pay you to purchase goods, to go into a certain pub and order a pre-determined round of drinks or to go to the cinema and see the latest film.

You then have to report back to the company facts about the shop or premises you visited, its staff, service and products. Some assignments even involve a free night in a hotel - but you'll need to start with the more mundane jobs and prove your worth before you get to do the exciting stuff.

### How much can you make?
Each job pays from about £6 to £20 plus expenses. How much work is available to you depends on fluctuations within the industry and how flexible you can be.

### Contacts
To get started, register with mystery shopping agencies such as Retail Rapport Ltd. (www.mysteryshopagency.com), IMS

(www.ukims.co.uk or telephone 0870 7010866) or Retaileyes (www.retaileyes.co.uk or telephone 01908 328000).

## 5. Invigilating exams

Invigilators ensure that school, college and university exams are carried out properly. They are also responsible for handing out question and answer sheets, making sure no one cheats and collecting papers at the end.

Local education authorities need invigilators for GCSE, A-level and university exams and for exams set under adult education programmes. The call is greatest for invigilators during January and June / July.

### How much can you make?
Invigilating for a three-hour exam pays about £45 but you will have to be there for an hour or so before and after the exam.

### Contacts
Contact your local education authority, school or university for more details.

## Case study

Rachel Newcombe, 31, is a freelance journalist from Devon who does mystery shopping for Retaileyes, ABA Research and Assosia (a retail monitoring and quality assurance organisation) to supplement her income.

She says: "I saw a company advertising for mystery shoppers and I thought it would be a rather fun way of earning some extra cash, whilst getting to shop at the same time. It fits in really well, especially as I'm already freelance and can be flexible with my hours.

"Living where I do, there's not a major demand for mystery shopping assignments, so they only tend to come up now and again."

The shopping Rachel has done varies. Some have been simple mystery shopping tasks: she had to go to a store on a particular day, ask the store assistants certain questions, maybe try some clothes on and then purchase them.

Others have involved having a meal at a particular restaurant and studying the service and ambience of the place. She has even had to conduct a mystery shopping audit at a large supermarket.

"As for pay, that varies too," says Rachel, "On average, for a simple 10 minute assignment, it's about £10, which isn't bad for an extra bit of cash. Usually, if you have to buy a particular product or item of clothing, that cost is reimbursed too."

## 6. House sitting

House-sitters look after people's houses, pets and plants while they are away on holiday, on a business trip or simply out for the day – favourite opportunities for burglars. Although you can do this on an informal basis for friends and family, joining an agency is best. www.housesitters.co.uk vets sitters carefully.

They also have to abide by a stringent set of rules that include not leaving the property for more than three hours at a time or for more than half an hour after dark.

For this reason, it's best suited to people without other work commitments, such as students on vacation or retired people.

### How much can you make?
Agencies pay between £120 and £150 a week but if you work independently it is up to you how much you charge.

### Contacts
Visit www.housesitters.co.uk or www.housesittersltd.co.uk to find out more about becoming a sitter.

---

### Wise Words
Many of the jobs you can find yourself don't require specialist skills. As with many things in life, a high dose of common sense, coupled with enthusiasm, will serve you well

# THE 25 WAYS
# Sell, sell, sell

7. **Selling things you don't want**

   A good clear out at home can mean you have a whole load of things to sell. These days you can either head down to the nearest car boot sale and do it in person, or advertise your goods in newspapers, newsagents' windows or on the internet.

   eBay is one of the internet's biggest phenomenons. While some people simply sell stuff they don't need any more, others set up online stores and make eBay their main source of income.

   For the uninitiated, you need to register and set up an account and can then list items you want to sell in the form of auctions where buyers bid for your items. A small proportion of every sale goes to eBay as a fee.

Watching people bid and out-bid each other for your unwanted gear is great fun and you can end up getting loads of money for something you thought was worthless.

### How much can you make?
How much you make depends on what you're selling, but people might pay a surprising amount for what you consider to be worthless. Be warned though, if you are running a full-time business on eBay, tax inspectors will make sure you pay tax on your earnings.

### Contacts
Check your local newspaper for boot sales or simply put an ad in the paper. Otherwise visit www.ebay.co.uk to sell almost anything or www.amazon.co.uk to sell books, videos, CDs and DVDs. For extra security, www.paypal.com offers an electronic wallet.

## 8. Direct selling
If you know your nail varnish from your lip balm, working for door-to-door cosmetics company, Avon, could be for you. Avon

## Case study

Andy Poole, 24, from Manchester, has been selling things he doesn't want any more on eBay to save money for his wedding next year. He says: "This has included selling a whole host of old household junk and I've posted items all over the world including the States, Australia, Germany, France and Belgium. In total, I've probably made about £400 profit in eight months."

recruits people to take on a sales territory and sell make-up and perfume on a commission basis. You can work your own hours and recruit other agents to make extra money.

Ann Summers, Kleeneze, and the Body Shop all run similar schemes. Phone operators such as Euphony also recruit part-time business consultants to bring in new customers.

### How much can you make?

While some sellers only earn a couple of hundred pounds a year, average annual earnings across the industry are £4-£5,000.

## Case study

As a student, Pete Wright registered with cut-rate landline telephone service provider Euphony. Euphony purchases bulk volumes of call minutes from landline network operators and resells them to residential and business customers at a low rate.

Pete started boosting his student income by working part-time for Euphony – and ended up selling for them as a full-time job.

### Contacts

www.dsa.org.uk lists companies that operate direct selling operations. Telephone 020 7497 1234.

www.avon.uk.com provides information on working for Avon and you can apply online.

www.thebodyshop.com contains details of how to host a Body Shop At Home party. Telephone 08459 050607.

# THE 25 WAYS
# Use your body

### 9. Take part in a police ID parade

Who says crime doesn't pay? Police stations regularly need people of all types to take part in police ID line-ups. Modern technology means police are using video-based line-ups more now. If they think they might need someone who looks like you, they will video you from all angles and add it to their library.

**How much can you make?**
One-off fees are £10 to £15.

**Contacts**
Contact your local police station.

## 10. Medical trials

These days you do not have to wait until you die to donate your body to science. Drugs, make-up and cold remedies all need to be tested on humans before they can go to market.

Studies range from a few hours to weeks. Live-in ones tend to provide facilities where you can read, play games, surf the internet, or watch TV and videos.

If you don't fancy being pumped full of drugs, psychological research might be for you instead. The tests normally involve brain scans, simple memory exercises or cognitive function studies

### How much can you make?
Live-in studies can pay several hundreds of pounds a week while psychological studies normally pay between £5 and £10 an hour.

### Contacts
The Covance clinical research unit (www.covance.com) is a world leading

research organisation which is always looking for participants.

Biotrax provides support, information and advice to people wishing to take part in clinical and psychological trials. www.biotrax.co.uk has links allowing you to apply for trials online after completing an eligibility test. Telephone 0161 736 7312.

Psychological experiments are often advertised in local papers, on student notice boards or at institutions such as Clinical Neuroscience Research in Dartford, Kent.

## 11. Dog walking

Many people are too busy to look after their pets as well as they would like, while some are out at work all day but feel Rover could do with a lunchtime walk. To get started, it is best to ask around your friends and neighbours to see if they need their dog walked, or advertise at the local vet's practice.

## How much can you make?

How much you make is up to you and depends on your clientele. Well-off businessmen with more money than time will pay more than elderly people no longer fit enough to keep up with their pet. Dog walkers in London charge £10 to £15 per dog.

## 12. Be a TV extra

Ricky Gervais' BBC hit 'Extras' has prompted many people to register with extras agencies in the hope they will be picked to sup a pint in The Rover's Return, wait in the reception in 'Casualty' or be part of a throbbing crowd in a Hollywood blockbuster.

There are a lot of agencies around, some good, some pretty dodgy, but you can check with the union BECTU (www.bectu.org.uk), 020 7346 0900 to find out if an agency is reputable. Extras, with or without acting experience, are needed from all walks of life.

Being flexible and available is useful, as is living in or near cities where TV dramas are made on a regular basis.

### How much can you make?
The basic pay is £64.50 a day but you can earn more if you have to do overtime, shoot at night, use your own special props or uniform or you have a special skill such as rollerblading or juggling.

### Contacts
London-based Casting Collective (www.castingcollective.co.uk) on 020 8962 0099 can register you as interested in TV extra work while www.supportingartists.com provides information about the industry.

## 13. Rent out a room
If you've got a spare room in your house or flat, renting it out can be the perfect way to get some extra income. Tax rules mean you can earn up to £4,250 a year tax-free.

Make sure you interview potential housemates first and are convinced of their ability to pay the rent. Also lay down some house rules – getting the right tenant is vital.

## How much can you make?
This depends on where in the country your house or flat is – you will be able to demand more rent in London, for example – how big the room you are renting out is, how close you are to transport and other amenities and the general state of your home.

## Contacts
For information on the Government's rent-a-room scheme, visit www.inlandrevenue.gov.uk To advertise a room, try www.loot.com or www.gumtree.com.

# THE 25 WAYS
# Space to Spare

### 14. Have an ad on your car

If you do not mind being a driving advert for a brand of some kind, having an advert splashed across your car could be for you. www.adsoncars.com gives details on how to go about it. Basically, companies pay you to promote their product on your car and then they apply artwork in a way that means it can be taken off easily later.

There are certain criteria to meet though. They may include having a particular age or type of car, living in the right area or doing a certain amount of mileage. Coca Cola, Mars,

Yahoo, Procter & Gamble, Jockey, Rowntrees, Cadburys, O2, Nikon, Carlsberg, Marmite and Vimto all use this kind of advertising.

## How much can you make?

Companies pay between £70 and £200 a month simply for driving around with an ad on your car. Sometimes they offer free petrol instead.

## Contacts

www.adsoncars.com has all the details and an online application form. Telephone 020 8906 6682 or 0845 2267724.

## 15. Using your home as a film or TV set

Almost every type of home is of interest to companies filming adverts, TV dramas and films. Amazing Space was established in 1994 and is run by a team of experienced coordinators.

Since then, it has found literally thousands of locations for feature films, television dramas and commercials and stills photography. Its credits include scenes in James Bond films, 'Bridget Jones' Diary' and 'Footballers' Wives'.

Different types of property are always required. They can vary from run-down bed-sits to stately homes, depending on the production. But places with big rooms, parking facilities and owners relaxed about crews of 30 or 40 people taking over their home are preferred.

## How much can you make?

Anything from £300 to £1,000 a day, depending on your property and what it is being used for. Shoots taking place over several days or weeks will pay more, but you will probably need to find alternative accommodation while film crews are in your home.

## Contacts

Amazing Space (telephone 020 7251 6661) at www.amazingspace.co.uk hosts the ultimate location library. You can add your property to it for a registration cost of £120.

Another company, Location Partnership (www.locationpartnership.com, telephone

020 7734 0456) scouts for film locations around the UK and worldwide. It's free to register but you have to pay the company 10 per cent commission if your home is used.

## 16. Negotiate a pay rise

So, you think you're coming up with the goods and are worth more money – but you're too scared to ask for a pay rise. Approaching the boss to ask for more cash can be nerve-wracking at the best of times but careful preparation can help negotiations go your way.

### How much can you make?

This depends on your current salary and how much extra you're asking for. Aim high and it is likely you will agree on a figure somewhere in the middle.

### Contacts

Check out the salary calculator on www.reed.co.uk to see what you should be earning in your profession.

## Expert tips

Joanna Roberts of Reed Employment says: "Asking for a pay rise is a business proposition and you should treat it as such. You need to convince your boss that it is worth making a financial investment in you – and make it clear how the organization will benefit from that investment.

"Make a formal appointment to talk to your boss, as this will let them know that you mean business. Prepare for your meeting by collecting evidence of ways in which your work has contributed to the organization's success.

"It is also worth thinking about what your boss is likely to say, so that you are prepared to counter any objections."

# THE 25 WAYS
# Making
# of what

### 17. Monthly income savings accounts

If you've got some cash saved up, then finding the right home for it can help boost your income. Monthly income accounts or bonds provide a monthly income, usually an interest payment.

Consulting an independent financial adviser is the best way to find the right account for you and your savings.

### How much can you make?

Basic savings accounts managed online normally pay about 5 per cent interest annually, so if you have got £10,000 savings you can get about £40 a month in interest. Longer-term investments or bonds pay more, but your money will be tied in for a set period.

# the most you've got

### Contacts
Visit www.unbiased.co.uk to find a financial adviser in your area, or call 0800 085 3250.

### 18. Tax credits

Tax credits are means-tested payments. Working parents may be able to claim two credits – child tax credit and working tax credit. To qualify for child tax credit you must be responsible for looking after at least one child.

Working tax credit is designed to top up the earnings of low-paid workers, and includes a childcare element for working parents. You must be employed or self-employed and in paid employment for at least 16 hours a week.

Tax credits are money you are entitled to, so it's worth checking out if you qualify for any. These type of credits have come in for some bad press recently: some people have been paid too much and HM Revenue & Customs have then clawed back the money.

## How much can you make?

As a rough guide, families with a household income of £30,000 to £50,000 could receive an annual child tax credit of £545, regardless of how many children they have. Those on an income of £20,000 could receive £645 for one child and £2,340 for two.

Payments to those on lower incomes or with disabled children are greater.

## Contact

Visit www.taxcredits.inlandrevenue.gov.uk to find out if you qualify for tax credits. You can fill in and submit a form online to see what you are entitled to. Or phone the tax credits helpline on 0845 300 3900.

## 19. Forgotten bank accounts

Apparently, between £15 and £20 billion lies languishing in unclaimed savings' accounts, pension funds, endowment policies, etc.

Accounts are classified as dormant when no transactions have been made for a set period (generally one year), or if a statement or other official correspondence is returned as undeliverable. After between one and three years, the funds are transferred to a reserve account, generally on low interest.

### How much can you make?
This depends on how much cash you've forgotten you had. As a nation, we have forgotten between £15 and £20 million, so who knows how much of it is yours?

### Contacts
Experian's Unclaimed Assets Register (www.uar.co.uk) is the only source that brings together data from a variety of financial institutions. It charges a flat fee of £18 to search for 'lost' policies and accounts.

# THE 25 WAYS
# Use your

## 20. DIY

If you're a dab hand with a screwdriver, drill or paintbrush, you could find there is a market for DIY skills in your area. People sometimes need help with small jobs like changing a fuse, putting flat pack furniture together or putting up a picture. A high proportion of these are single women who need a 'husband' for the day.

While plumbing and electrical work is best left to the professionals, DIY skills are very much in demand.

### How much can you make?

Generally, you can make about £20 to £40 an hour, depending on your skills, who your customers are (you might want to charge elderly people less, for example) and where you live.

# Skills

### Contact
An ad in your local newsagent can get things moving, as can advertising your services through word-of-mouth. Papers like Friday Ad (www.friday-ad.co.uk) or Loot (www.loot.com) also carry adverts for odd-job men.

## 21. Be a therapist
Massage is becoming more popular all the time, as people seek to escape from the stresses and strains of everyday life. There are also a growing number of alternative therapies around, such as hypnotherapy, aromatherapy and reflexology. Each treats different physical and psychological conditions.

Although ultimately rewarding, getting qualified as a masseur is time-consuming and expensive. You could need to spend a year and £1,500 to £2,000 getting qualified before you can even start making any money. There are exams too, both practical and written and you will need to hit the books to pass.

> **"Although ultimately rewarding, getting qualified as a masseur is time-consuming and expensive"**

### How much can you make?
Once qualified, massage therapists charge £20 to £45 an hour. But you'll need to make some investment too. Massage courses don't come cheap and you will also need a massage table, oils and maybe a uniform.

### Contacts
There are a lot of courses around for masseurs and therapists. The London-based Institute for Complementary Medicine (www.icmedicine.co.uk)

on 020 7237 5165 or the Massage Training Institute (www.massagetraining.co.uk) can provide more details.

## "If you've got good secretarial skills and can fit in work around your other commitments, being a virtual PA could be for you"

### 22. Be a virtual PA

Some businesses don't need a full time PA or secretary but just need help with admin every now and again. As a result, more and more PAs and secretaries are opting to go solo – setting up away from the office or as freelance secretaries – and have coined the phrase 'virtual PA' or simply 'VA'.

Some offer admin services via email, fax and telephone or it might be occasional typing or chasing suppliers and payments. If you've got good secretarial skills and can fit in work around your other commitments, being a virtual PA could be for you.

### How much can you make?
How much you make is up to you but typical rates are £10 to £20 an hour for typing. If you offer a call answering service, you might charge per call or a flat hourly rate.

### Contact
www.needmoretime.co.uk gives examples of the services virtual PAs offer. The International Association of Virtual Assistants (www.iava.org.uk) can give you ideas for how to get started and provide a network of VAs.

## Case study
Andrew Lewis, 34, trained as a reflexologist at weekends last year, alongside his day job as an account manager in an events and training company. He spent about £1,000 on a reflexology course.

**THE 25 WAYS: Use your Skills**

He also had to pass one written exam, carry out two supervised practical one-hour treatments and undertake and document 60 hours of treatments on a series of six clients over an eight-month period of practical assessments.

Andrew says: "I have always been interested in alternative therapies, and feet, and I thought being a reflexologist would be rewarding and interesting as well as helping to heal people".

At the moment Andrew is just starting out and sees one or two or clients a week. He charges them £35.00 for an hour's treatment in his home or £45 an hour if he has to travel to them.

"I find the extra money useful and I enjoy it – sometimes it can be hard work and other times it isn't. It really depends on the client and my own energy levels – especially after being in the office doing my day job."

# THE 25 WAYS
# Use your

### 23. Invent a game show

The inventors of ITV's 'Who Wants To Be A Millionaire?' have made millions for turning a simple idea into an award-winning concept. TV production companies are always on the look out for the next big thing to get viewers hooked.

Before you get started, make sure to watch lots of game shows. Nothing will scupper your plans quicker than if, after weeks of development, you later discover that a show working along identical lines is already on air.

Next, you need to think of a basic idea around which your whole show will revolve, and develop it with your audience in mind. You should be able to fit its format onto one or two sheets of A4 paper. Anything longer, and it's probably too complicated.

# imagination

Pitching it around production companies and TV channels such as Celador is your next step in making it onto screen.

### How much can you make?
If your idea is accepted, then be prepared to negotiate.

### Contacts
www.bbc.co.uk/talent shows opportunities in TV and is all about finding new talent rather than people with qualifications.

Celador (www.celador.co.uk) makes 'Who Wants To Be A Millionaire?', 'The People Versus' and 'Winning Lines'. Contact it on 020 7845 6999.

'Big Brother' maker Endemol is also worth checking out at www.endemol.com.

## 24. Sell stories to newspapers

Big news events in 2005 have spawned the rise of 'citizen journalism'; that is, members of the public supplying newspapers and agencies with words and pictures. The press snapped up video clips of the Asian tsunami and pictures taken on mobile phones of the 7/7 bombs. They were looking for images of the moment that disaster struck.

You don't need to be on the scene of a major catastrophe to make some extra cash, though. Spotting celebrities out and about and reporting back to newspaper gossip columns about what they're up to, who they're with and where they're eating and drinking can make you some easy money.

Meanwhile, www.scoopt.com launched last year and acts as a broker selling photos taken by members of the public to the mainstream media.

**THE 25 WAYS: Use your imagination**

## How much can you make?
It depends; spotting celebrities arguing in Tesco might earn you £50. A member of the public who videoed the arrests of the terror suspects who tried to bomb London on July 21 is rumoured to have earned a five-figure sum for his camera work.

## Contacts
Visit Scoopt at www.scoopt.com for more information on selling photographs, or contact editors of national newspapers directly.

Email The Sun newsdesk on news@thesun.co.uk or call it on 020 7782 4100.

The Mirror has offices in London and Manchester on 020 7293 3831 and 0161 683 6402 respectively, or can be emailed on mirrornews@mgn.co.uk. If you've spotted someone famous, call The Mirror's 3am girls on 020 7293 3950 or email 3am@mirror.co.uk.

## 25. Take part in a TV game show
From Jim Bowen uttering the immortal

mantra, "super smashing great" to Ann Robinson telling hapless contestants, "you are the weakest link, goodbye", TV game shows have captivated the nation's attention. Big prize jackpots are becoming more and more commonplace, turning ordinary people into millionaires overnight.

Programmes with big prizes include 'Who Wants To Be A Millionaire?' (£1m), 'The Weakest Link' (£10k) and 'In It To Win It' (£100k). Lower budget productions, such as 'Brainteaser' and 'Memorybank', offer smaller prizes but are generally easier to get on to.

## How much can you make?
Answer 15 questions correctly in a row on 'Millionaire' and you will be just that, while contestants on 'Brainteaser' can walk away with anything from £100 to £3,000.

## Contacts
Websites www.ukgameshows.com and www.quizzing.co.uk both include lists of shows currently needing contestants.

# Another approach

It's no good spending hours thinking of ways to boost your income if you're wasting what you *do* have on everyday expenses. A simple re-organization of your finances can result in having more cash to spend each month and leave you safe in the knowledge that you're not lining the pockets of fat cats at the helm of big companies.

There are about 7,000 mortgage products on the market at any one time and so it's likely that if you haven't remortgaged lately, you're on the wrong deal. A couple of hours spent shopping around on the internet might save you hundreds each month.

Most mortgages have a fixed or discounted period where you pay a preferable rate. After that, you switch to the lender's standard variable rate (SVR), which will be over the base rate.

Remortgaging is not as time-consuming or costly as most consumers think. In reality, shopping around for a new deal is pretty easy and the process could be complete in under a month.

Websites such as www.charcolonline.co.uk and www.moneysupermarket.com provide mortgage wizards tailored to each specific customer type – for example, first-time buyers or remortgagers.

This enables consumers to run targeted, personalised comparisons to find the best deal for them. Customers can apply online for some deals.

If you are not internet-savvy, or would prefer to receive professional advice, a mortgage broker can help. Around half of all the mortgages in the UK are arranged by a broker or adviser.

If you're in debt with either credit cards or personal loans, shopping around could also bag you a better deal. Lots of credit cards have 0 per cent deals now, where, for a set amount of time, you don't pay an interest on either balance transfers or new purchases.

Switching your existing debt to one of these cards can stop interest charges racking up and help you pay off the balance more quickly. Similarly, there are personal loans around these days with rates as low as 5.8 per cent, so if you're paying more than that on your loan, it will be worth changing.

Websites such as www.uswitch.com and www.moneysupermarket.com can help you compare credit cards and loans as well as other financial products.

Electricity and gas companies have been hiking their prices over the past couple of years. If you haven't switched supplier recently, you could probably benefit from doing so. Consumers can opt for separate companies to provide gas and electricity or for one company to supply both.

Internet-based comparison services such as www.simplyswitch.com, www.firsthelpline.com or www.ukpower.co.uk will compare the different services for you and arrange the changeover.

All you need to do is type in your address, your current supplier, annual or monthly charge and some details about your living arrangements. The site will then list alternative suppliers, prices and, in some cases, service ratings. If you've never switched supplier before, you could save about £170 a year.

## "If you've never switched supplier before, you could save about £170 a year"

Similarly if you haven't switched home phone provider for some time, you'll find lots of companies are cheaper than BT. You still need a BT line in order to use many cheap call operators but there are some good packages around which include all landline calls for under £10 a month.

Alternatively, internet-based prefix number www.call18866.com only charges 3p per call to a UK landline, regardless of the length of the call.

Likewise, many people pay over the odds for using their mobile phone. Most tariffs come with a number of talk minutes and text messages included each month, but costs can rise sharply if you go over this amount.

To get a better deal, compare tariffs on www.onecompare.com or simply call your provider, say you are thinking of cancelling your contract and negotiate a better deal. Most will match the cheapest deals around and you won't have to go through the hassle of changing your provider. Most will upgrade your handset too.

For some purchases, shopping online can reap rewards. Shopbots (internet search engines for comparing on-line prices) or shopping robots such as www.Kelkoo.co.uk or www.shopping.com search the internet for you and compile tables of the cheapest sites to buy products.

The biggest savings are to be found on widescreen TVs and digital cameras. You'll save an average of 23 and 26 per cent respectively, says Which?

**25 ways to BOOST your income**

Even if you're only buying cheaper things like CDs and DVDs you might find them cheaper on the internet. Sites such as CDWow! (www.cdwow.com) sell chart CDs for £6.99 compared to about £9.99 on the high street.

## Quick123
•GUIDES TO EVERYTHING•

### Got an idea for a new topic?

**Drop us a line:**
Email: ideas@quick123.co.uk
Post: Quick123 Limited,
PO Box 45092, London N4 2ZJ

# And finally

The ideas in this book are not just income generators. They can also be fun and rewarding in other ways too.

Some will mean you meet new people, go to places you have never been to before or do things you have never done before. Others will allow you to use things you already have, such as skills and qualifications, to fulfil your money-making quest.

So what are you waiting for? Get started, get motivated and get going.

25 ways to BOOST your income

# Further

• • • • • • • • • • • • • • • • • • • • • • • • • • • •

**Updates to this guide can be found at:**
**www.quick123.co.uk/boost**

### A Bit on the Side:
### 500 ways to boost your income

by Jasmine Birtles. Published by Piatkus Books 2004/5, £10.99. This book is full of suggestions of how to make some extra cash. Some are easy, some unusual. It is illustrated by success stories and packed with information.

### How to sell anything on eBay
### and make a fortune

by Dennis L Prince. Published by McGraw Hill, £5.99. This is the definitive guide to allow you to consistently get the highest bids and happiest customers on the internet's best known auction site.

**Further reading**

# reading

## Make Money, Be Happy: How to Make All the Money You Want, Doing What You Want to Do

by Carmel McConnell. Published by Financial Times Prentice Hall, £6.99. Make Money, Be Happy shatters the myth that you have to choose between healthy finances and happiness. It shows that, whatever your starting point, it is possible to have both.

## The Money Diet: The Ultimate Guide to Shedding Pounds Off Your Bills and Saving Money on Everything!

by Martin Lewis. Published by Vermilion. £7.99. Written by the award-winning creator of www.moneysavingexpert.com, this book shows you how to cut your bills without cutting back.

**The Motley Fool** at www.fool.co.uk. One of the web's best guides to financial products and getting out of debt.

# Also available from

# Quick123™
### • GUIDES TO EVERYTHING •

- Get a Good Night's Sleep
- How to Protect Yourself from Identity Theft
- 25 Ways to Boost Your Income
- Get Started On eBay
- Get Out of Debt - and stay out
- Lose a Stone - and keep it off

and many more.....

For a list of titles and products go to
www.quick123.co.uk